THE AWAKENING OF KAFFEINE KOFFEE

BY OBELLA

Table of Contents

INTRODUCTION 12

Human rights is dead...14

Earthlings..14

Recycle black children (foster care)......................................14

European Union...15

Christians 15

Negro Native American 15

Terror/being displaced 16

THE REAL JEWS 16

Negro manifesto...16

Discontinuing Michigan Human Services for people 17

Mass transit 18

Native Americans 18

Uprooting 18

Gun violence..19

Love 19

America land of the abused...19

Lottery 20

Bias 20

The enemy from within 21

Good woman 21

Love 21

America the new Babylon 22

Church 22

Lucifer TV show 22

Complicated world 22

Destroyers 23

Emergency managers 23

Government answering machines 23

People of color 23

New Ideology 24

Sell outs 24

MDHHS-Medicaid 24

The ballot of the people's choice 25

Wakeup 25

Political Bully's 26

Immigrants get better perks 26

Immigrants in the country 26

Melting Pot 27

Black people frustrated 27

RACISM 27

Pray for America 28

Student loans 28

Dignity 28

Greedy politicians 29

Honor 29

Political chess 29

Marijuana Ordinance 29

State surplus 29

Raggedy old houses 30

Capitalism 30

White people standup 30

Broken Covenant 30

Immigration 30

White Education 30

WE HOLD THESE TRUTHS 31

Jew is not a RACE 31

White politicians...32

Michigan State Police (racial profiling) 32

Allegiance 33

Lottery 33

Relationships 33

Religion 34

Flint water crisis Lead 34

Soulfulness 34

Classless...34

Socialization of the Blackman...35

Desocialization of Negro's in America 35

High morals Black women and Blackman.............................35

Corrupted Lottery...36

GUN CONTROL!!!!!!!!! 36

Negro's standup!! 37

Charity all Year long..37

It's time to stop with being the ignorant black woman........37

Urban Entitlements 38

Outsourcing and Overpricing...38

Jesus the JEW?..38

A letter to Ben Carson 38

False Allegiance 39

Smoking Weed...40

Help others 40

Part of the problem 40

GODLY...40

China free healthcare 40

Boycott Whitehouse 41

Americas in a crisis 41

American Dream Foreigners..41

Ungodly things..42

God power..43

Economical bondage 43

Pipeline to Jail...43

Trick or treat...43

Weed 43

Trumpism 44

Capitalism 44

Protect and Serve 44

Insurance corruption 45

Richer or Poorer 45

America's Arab, Indian, Chinese businesses in the Black communities 45

Diana Ross 46

Moral responsibility..46

Healthcare wall street commodity 47

Mandatory healthcare...47

Corrupt credit score agencies...47

Middle Class 47

America's Enslavement 48

Good morning 48

Obamacare 48

Get thee behind me..49

Rapping is Poison 49

Don't Rock the Boat "OBAMA 49

Where's the POPE...50

Hidden Figures...50

Republican Conspiracy: The WALL 51

Adoption of black children by Whites is wrong..........................51

It is Written..51

Down with the two-party systems 53

Politicians or Murders 53

Democrats and Republicans Enemies of the People 53

Fake Lottery System 54

Political Mess...54

Imperialism vs Capitalism 54

ADVOCATE FOR POVERTY..55

Social Services blackout...55

Difference between democrats/republicans.........................56

MDHHS Mission...56

Diversify the Supreme Court Justice..................................58

Justice 58

Malcolm X Chickens comes home to Roost...........................58

KNEELING BEFORE THE PLEDGE 59

PTSD 59

LOVE 59

LIFE 60

Drugs Destroy 60

Pledge of Allegiance 60

Military Upset WHY? 61

Pledge of Allegiance (Quote) 61

Melody 63

Crystal..63

Political Cowards 63

Negro Morals..63

Political Cowards 64

NEGRO MORALS 64

We need a Hero...64

Confessions..65

Down with Democrats Republicans.................................65

Thou shall not KILL..65

Florence...65

Justice is dead...66

Racism/Poverty 66

Lawless 66

Child support 67

Humans 67

Drugs 67

America legalized Sodomy..67

Diversity..68

Confessions...68

DOWN with the Democrats, Republicans.........................68

Babylon in America...69

White vs Black 69

4th of July 69

Government corruption 70

AWAKE..70

Sin 70

Love thyself 70

Christian values 71

No mass transportation...71

REVIEW CROSS RACIAL FOSTERING/ADOPTION 71

Don't Apologize 71

Generation of being privilege/Whiteman 72

Legislate Justice for All 72

White people and hatred 72

GOD'S MANY NAMES 73

Under Siege in America 73

Poverty 73

Crime 73

New World Order 74

Free healthcare and free education 74

Self Esteem 74

The WORD 74

Wages of Sinning 75

Self-Supporting 75

False Christians 75

Ridiculous USDA American Harvest Box 75

FDA/PRESCRIPTION DRUGS CORRUPTION 76

Difference between ground and surface water(Quote) 76

Evil people in Whitehouse 77

Fake News by Russia 77

BLACK HISTORY 77

Proud Mary's 77

Labeling of Religion 78

Spirit of God Spirit of God 78

U.S. tax dollars 79

Difference in Race vs Culture 79

Equality 79

Negroid 79

Tribes 79

Manhood and Womanhood 80

Spirit of GOD 80

Government shutdown 80

Black men and Black female relationships 80

Russia's Assimilates in America 81

Veterans 81

Martin Luther King..82

Leaders 82

POOR VS WEALTHY..82

Desocialization/Criminalizing 83

Decriminalize Yourself 83

Rapping vs Singing 83

Electoral votes 83

ABOUT THE AUTHOR 85

FUTURE BOOKS BY THE AUTHOR 86

INTRODUCTION

THE AWAKENING OF KAFFEINE KOFFEE

THIS IS ABOUT THE EVENTS THAT ARE TAKING PLACE IN OUR SOCIETY OF TODAY.THESE VERSES ARE TO LET YOU KNOW OF HOW AMERICA IS NOT TAKING RESPONSIBILITY FOR THE ILLS OF OUR SOCIETY.WE NEED T CONSCIOUSLY EXAMINE WHAT IS HAPPENING IN OUR WORLD OF TODAY, FOR A BETTER FUTURE AND WORLD.I CAN FORESEE A BRIGHTER DAY BY CONSCIOUSLY LETTING YOU KNOW WHAT PROBLEMS ARE GOING ON IN OUR WORLD TODAY,AND I TRULY GIVE YOU MY BEST OPINION OF WHAT NEEDS TO BE DONE!WE ARE IN AN AGE OF PERILOUS TIMES IN WHICH WE AS HUMANS HAVE TO SLOW DOWN AND BECOME AWARE OF WHAT IS HAPPENING IN A SOCIETY THAT STILL PREACHES MORE HATE THAN LOVE.AND LAWS ARE CHANGING TO PROTECT THE

WEALTHY AND NOT THE POOR.WE MUST BRING BACK LOVE TO OVERSHADOW THE HATE THAT HAS MANIFEST OVER CENTURIES.WE MUST BRING BACK THE GODLINESS OF OUR SAVIOR AND THE HUMAN RACE,AND AMEND LAWS TO PROTECT THE PEOPLE AND NOT JUST THE WEALTHY ONES.

BY OBELLA (AUTHOR)

Human rights is dead

I am ashamed of the state and local leaders around the country, that are not providing poor black people and some poor white people, the right to receive services from the Human Services Dept in each state, such as food stamps, utility payments, shelter payments, clothing vouchers, things to keep the people unemployed means and way to survive, so that they want to have to make other people victims and end up in jail! The people didn't create poverty, the politics and the wealthy did! But we suffer from their selfish, corrupt minds of being ignorant and racist! Can't you see how the young black men are letting their hair grow out at the disparity of being in a society that is not providing good social welfare for the community. Shame on you leaders of the community and the states government and federal entities! Human rights are dead!

Earthlings

Earthlings, study war no more. I put you on earth to enjoy the fruits of your own labor, and to be fruitful and multiply. There is no need to have war against your fellowman. Stop destroying Africa and other countries with war. The terrorist needs jobs and education in their own lands and they will be terrorist no more. There will be no need to immigrate people to other countries. Build within your own countries for PEACE! América rebuild urban cities and stop destroying blacks within your own country. This was not what I created Earth for! Correct the error of your ways and I will come in peace!

Recycle black children (foster care)

A good way to recycle the black children in America is to shut the doors of social services and cut food stamps, and don't offer jobs nor apprenticeship programs to the families and keep the fathers away through unemployment, so that the children want to have stable homes. This leads to neglect and abuse, so guess what white child and family agencies keep their jobs, judges, attorneys keep their jobs, white social workers keep their jobs, because we need them to set up placements for the children, because they feel it's cheaper rather than reunite the kids and keep them in their own biological homes with families! DUMB

European Union

European Union, what's next. America has been displacing blacks for years, letting these white immigrants come into our country, and removing the blacks from their minority status, in which we fought and died NACCP knew what was happening, and does not support our minority causes any longer. Black people we need a Universal Black Union so that we can protect persons of color, and establish funds to fight against this global racism, that's keeping us economically oppressed!

Christians

I'm confused! If white Christians are believers of the Lord Jesus Christ. Then why do they continue to defy his teachings and laws as it is written in the bible. And dissuade other religions such as for instance Muslims from practicing what their GOD preaches! Can I get a witness! Men

Negro Native American

The Negro in America is a native of America, not Africa. We have been displaced and treated badly in our own country and have been made to feel like we belong to Africa, but that's not true. This country is our country, we are natives of this country, and we need to start acting like it! Our children are wearing their hair long or marking themselves trying to look like the white establishment. That's what the evilness of these white Christians are doing to my people. We don't ask for much, just to live equally and peacefully. Is this too much to ask for, white Christians.

Terror/being displaced

Theory! Everybody knows when you foster or adopt children most of the children at some point in time rebel against you and literally hate you, no matter how much therapy they receive. So, the same situation occurs when you displace people from their homelands. The government reaches out to the immigrants but trust me they view you as their enemy. This is what is happening now in America, and it's not necessarily going to be caused by the terrorist group. This is stored self-defiance that reaches out for satisfaction of being displaced by separation of war or neglected by the government!

THE REAL JEWS

Believe it are not! The true Jews are the people of color. The Gentiles are the white people of the earth. The Jews that are white people are of the Gentile race. Gentile meaning "feminine", that's why their race is more changeable in gender than any other race. Any race with Caucasian skin is a Gentile. It is written!

Negro manifesto

Negro Manifesto of living in America! To the white people, to the Chinese people, to the Indian people, to the Arab people and any other nation of people who think they are better than the Negro. Ever since America was founded we have been living in fear and made to fight in your wars to battle your enemies, there were Negro's fighting under your command in the Revolutionary war, Civil war, World War I and II, Korean War, Vietnam War, Gulf War, etc and we still get no respect. We have n... ever been at war with the Whiteman or any other nationality. All we want is for you the Whiteman to respect us and help us build unity within our own communities, just like what you expect for yourselves and families. We have contributed a lot to the welfare of America. We helped you build this nation. So, to all you white politicians voting on educational funds and social welfare funds that we need for our communities. I want you to think Chinese businesses and all the foreigners that you let immigrant to this country and make money from the Negro communities.

You constantly do a disservice to a group of people, that helped built America and got nothing in return. And you allowed the white Indians to disinherit a lot of Negro Indians from land because they were not white enough to fit into the scheme of what you had planned for the Trail of Tears! We don't want your pity; we want to be treated EQUAL! You also allowed millions of Negroes to be disinherited by the white slaveowners white descendants, so that the bi-racial descendants would not continue the generations of wealth! So, I ask you Whiteman, what is your problem of still denying the Negro the right to live as a HUMAN-BEING!

Discontinuing Michigan Human Services for people

I have reasons to believe that the Michigan Human Services dept is not servicing the city of Detroit citizens. You never hear anything about what resources you can get from them. We are hearing those children are homeless and the parents don't care. What is Wayne County Child and Family services mission and responsibility to protect these children, have they closed too. The governor of this state has shut down all social services for the Detroit community. This is the same thing Engler did to mental health. Where are the advocates for social injustice?

Food Stamps were cut, and the people are living in poor conditions, while downtown is booming of our tax dollars and the lottery revenue! People wake up!

Mass transit

Do we really have to have a debate in this city on whether we need MASS TRANSIT or not! This is the future of this city and every other city in America! Everybody can't afford high insurance premiums nor an automobile. Also, we need this to commute across the state for employment opportunities, after closing a lot of businesses due to selling out our jobs overseas to other countries, the government should be responsible and pay for it, so that we can easily commute to each city and travel. This is the future just like skyping on the cell phones. Dummies, invest in America!

Native Americans

Sermon for today! Something your ministers need to tell you! Negro's of America we are "NATIVE American's born and bred in this country! There is nothing wrong with using this term. Don't let the white race define you!

Uprooting

Although this was a very tragic loss, the news media needs to stop falsifying information about this was the largest massacre in American history. Also, America goes into other countries with war and displaces those immigrants from their countries and offer them asylum in America. Don't the government understand, you can uproot the people from their homeland, but the longing from whence they came will remain with them for the rest of their lifes,and the elders pass this down to the children and the children grow up hating America still! A time bomb waiting to go off! It's not about religion either! It's about families being destroyed!

Gun violence

Question! Has America set the stage for all this gun violence, by loose regulations, and to liberal with what they are letting producers put on mostly all crime movies on cable, every damn day for the children and people to watch! They have made us desensitize to violence and feed the minds of the mentally ill!

Love

This government needs to show the people how to love each other, rather than hate each other. This can be done by making better social programs and resources for the people and deprogram violence from the television networks!

America land of the abused

Sermon for today! White people in America such as Senator McCain and Trump want to always try to blame the black president for their white predecessors' mistakes. Well not true. Now that ISIS is the new terror, well let me tell you what I have notice. White people love war, and they keep blacks in their own native country of America in economical slavery by practicing racism and unequal opportunities to grow as a community. It's gotten so bad as to a system of foster care and adoption ...was set up because of the lack of economical funds that make black families neglect their families and responsibilities. This is displacement of the black family, and this causes post-traumatic stress in the black communities and the people are turning on each other, and the children are acting out killing one another and crime which leds them to prison. So I got to thinking about America always warring with other countries, because the dictatorship of those countries are not up to standard of how

America wants them to treat their own people. So they engage in sending our young men over to fight for those people such as in Iraq,Syria,Afghanistan ,libya,etc all for the sake of oil, or poppyseeds, to control for their own political gain. Then they displace and kill millions for this greed, and then want to use America as the foster parent for all these immigrants that they have destroyed their country. Then they get mad when the Muslims group sponsor terrorists in order to keep foreigners off their soil. In the meantime, when the immigrants hit our soil, the government irresponsibly don't check out the health or mental health of these people. Naturally when you are uprooted from your homeland, you will always carry a grudge against your oppressors! This has nothing to do with the mindset of ISIS's or ISIL. You would think the white politicians would know this! Instead, they want to blame Obama as usual! I don't see them letting millions of peaceful poor Negro Africans into this country!

Lottery

We give so much money to the States Lotteries and we don't ask for accountability or get a decent percentage back. We are a nation of stupidity! And I am included. We allow some asshole to review the computer to see how the odds are and they cheat by putting the number that they want to win, instead of just letting the numbers that come up just fall without evaluation of the odds! The State Commissioner have so many games out there, they can't even keep up with counting the monies!

Bias

I would like to know why the news media and crazy white politicians keep trying to insinuate that our president doesn't care about what's happening in Belgium. Why should he stop his trip to Cuba? Why don't they question the prime minister of Brussels and ask what they are going to do with their situation for the safety of Brussels. Our President has no control over what happens in another country! You should be glad it's not happening here! The media didn't ask Bush to rush to Katrina, Haiti, nor Kenya when all the disasters that occurred to Blacks. I hope Obama enjoys his stay in Cuba!

The enemy from within

Theory! You go over to a country that you believe declared war on your country! You send service men, and they wipe out that country, so many die! Then the war stops and all along you let the immigrants from that country come into this country and you help them gain businesses in the minority communities, but those minority people and the community you destroy, by not helping these people grow economically to support their own communities, and this causes crime to increase, because these minorities can't become self-sufficient and productive, because you the government is not offering ethic enclavement like you give immigrants, and we are the true Americans. So now you help these immigrants that you declared war on their country come and gain power in this country and now you wonder who funding ISIS is. Oh you know, you just don't want to admit it!

Good woman

A good woman or man will not allow conflict to continue within a family, they will show their love and understanding in making you do the right thing! If they allow conflict to exist, then you don't need that person in your life

Love

When you love someone, and they become confused to the issues of how to handle negative situations of life. You can believe it or not, that if someone truly loves you and have your best interest at heart, they will do everything in their power to help you, and not continually see you confused on issues that you don't want to believe is happening around you. Don't push away these people in order to satisfy the person that is only using you. Time will tell!

America the new Babylon

Question for today, is America the new Babylon, due to all the trash that they are allowing on television shows such as Scandal, How to get away with murder, and allowing all this gay bullshit of people feeling that gay people have a right to sin and adopt children teaching the kids that this is the correct way of life. This is bullshit! They are ruining America!

Church

If the Church believed in GOD, then why are they silently accepting all this immoral behavior that is being allowed to happen in our society! They have no voices anymore!

Lucifer TV show

Question! I wonder if any producer can write a show displaying "Christ", and make him the superhero trying to fight against the evils of mankind. They have balls enough to create a show about "Lucifer", fighting for justice. Give me a break! Brainwashing at its best! But at least they show Lucifer as being white! Right on! Don't the Whiteman get it, there is no salvation in being racist!

Complicated world

Black people, we live in a white world that is making it more sinful and complicated to live in! So we must join hands to protect our civil rights more now than ever before! We must stand up and fight for our civil rights and children of the now and future!

Destroyers

The Whiteman was put here to destroy the earth, as you can see by his continued effort to make racism a superpower to destroy persons of color! He does not come in peace!

Emergency managers

The governor's found out how to hide behind black emergency managers so that while they destroyed our urban cities, through economical starvation, the people could not yell racism! My problem is to where all the black leaders and professionals such as civil rights attorneys, who can go to court and file a mass class action lawsuit. They have given the Arab Chaldean our neighborhoods and shut the minority rights door right in our face. So that we no longer have banks to get loans from and the SBA is on the same page! The states and the federal government are in this together! We can sue and win! They have a right to offer ethnic enclavement to the black communities, just like they gave it to the immigrants and Jews, and Arabs!

Government answering machines

The United States government and the States have removed people from answering telephones and replaced them with automatic answering machines so that they don't have to account to the people of why we are not getting services! In Michigan this has grown so quickly at MDHHS and State offices, that you need to get help from, and no one returns or answers the phones.

People of color

People of color can't continue to live under the capitalist ideology, because it uses racism to keep us from raising economically in our communities. It is time to change over to a democracy that practices socialist ideology that is good for all mankind! Capitalism is not for the middle class nor the poor. It is for the wealthy and political party that wants to profit from our misery!

New Ideology

I'm not telling you how to vote but people we need new blood and an new ideology such as democratic socialism, due to the unfairness that the existing parties have shown to not help Blacks at all in completing in a country as first class citizens, and has placed us in a position to be living as a 3rd class citizen. They treat Arab-Chaldeans and other immigrants better than they treat their own Black citizens! Let's jump over Hillary and vote for honesty and truth through Bernie Sanders and ignore Donald Trump the clown!

Sell outs

Hillary and Bill sold our jobs to China and Mexico and anywhere they could help the big corporations get cheap labor. This speaks for itself and Bill with scandal after scandal, we don't need this. We need someone who is honest and truthful and cares about all people.

MDHHS-Medicaid

The person directing the MDHHS programs such as Michigan Medicaid programs and public health, Behavioral Health and Developmental disabilities is asleep and not taking care of making sure the subordinates under him is doing the job probably under Governor's Snyder's leadership. MEDICAID is in trouble, because the leadership in Wayne County is not training their workers how to input the Medicaid programs for the categorically and medically needed!

The ballot of the people's choice

The ballot in Michigan showed that we want a change. Congratulations BERNIE SANDERS. The young and the old people want a new ideology. We are sick and tired of the old corrupted democratic-capitalist and the republican-capitalist, they are the ones who sold our jobs and banks to the foreigners such as China and Mexico. We need a party that's for the people such as democratic socialism! The U.K. and all Europe practices Socialism and have free healthcare and education. Why not America! Look at Sweden, that is why we have news blackouts about these countries, because they don't want you to see how good they are living!

Wakeup

We must wake up and realize, we as blacks in America are living in perilous times! The State of Michigan as I see it is under leadership, which is conspiring to sabotage our black communities, by destroying our education dept of DPS, by not servicing the people through MDHHS, by letting the directors not show accountability for Wayne County Dept of Social services. They the workers are overloaded with cases and refuse to service the black communities by constantly denying cases that should be approved! Medicaid is being denied to people because the workers are not trained properly per each category that fits the persons situation. The lottery is discriminating with the educational fund do to they claim they give 100%, but Detroit is not getting one penny! Also, social services funds are being diverted to the Arab Chaldean Dearborn offices, so this means less funds are being used for our black neighborhoods. The young black children that graduate or drop out don't have any paid apprenticeship programs to get into, that leads to crime. This is how they are letting us destroy ourselves governor of this state has not done one damn thing to help the communities out since he been in office. The Mayor has not done anything but take the demolition money, but you got him crying broke ,but no demolitions have been done in these blighted neighborhoods, we got 99% white state policeman, and not one of our congressman said one damn thing about this discrimination. I'm sick and tired of all these professional house N**Gas sitting in jobs of authority and not doing one damn thing about these problems. Our minority status has been stolen by the Arab Chaldean, or later there will be a scandal in the Wayne County Treasurer office due to all of the commercial property having double parcels listed for the takeover someone else property that has not been cleared.

Political Bully's

Trump is a Bully type of personality and not mature enough to become the president! The white policeman that are providing us with protection is not man enough to stand up for justice when they see a black person being attacked by other white people, they are not worthy of being our protectors in the communities and black cops need to take a stand when they see their own kind being mistreated. You just don't turn the other cheek!

Immigrants get better perks

It seems to me the immigrants get better perks than naturalized citizens. The politicians write bills to bring them in so that they can undermine our economy through cheap labor! That's not good for the minorities or the middle class!

Immigrants in the country

Politicians think that bringing immigrants to this country going to solve their cost-of-living problems. So instead of paying other countries for cheap labor, they feel that it's smart to allow them to come here so that they can work for cheap labor, because the ceiling on wages is just too high for the profits the companies want to make! That's why Capitalism must go it does not work!

We need a democratic socialist ideology! This was predicted by Karl Marx!

Melting Pot

America is supposed to be the greatest melting pot in the world with a large, diversified race and ethnicities of people, who want to live together and love one another. So why is the politicians like Mr. Trump trying to use issues to separate this great nation. Together we stand, divided we fall. Race should not be an issue in this modern day and time! We must disavow Mr.Trump, he is not good for America! We must put a much greater human in charge of our country, such as "Bernie Sanders".

Black people frustrated

Young blackmen, I know you are frustrated, due to how America is treating you! But at this moment, the deportation of migrant workers is not your fight. Let the Mexican and immigrants take up their own stand! So please just chill, we have a bigger fight with racism in this country. We have to fight for paid apprenticeship programs for our youngblackmen so that they can become employed and not have a pipeline to prison! Let the immigrants complain about deportation! As you can see most of the politicians come from immigrants!

RACISM

White people stop being in denial, back in the day when America was still young, you were living under socialism due to the fact a lot of immigrants migrated to America, and they had nothing. So, you practice a socialist system at that time to upgrade your people to independence of a free enterprise by having welfare agencies created to provide for you people that they in turn could establish banks and institutions to become capitalist. So why suddenly you expect black people and poor whites to survive without these social norms such as welfare and free healthcare want them to survive being poor under a capitalist ideology to live or die. We can't compete with zip code racism, racial racism, insurance racism, credit score racism, high mortgage rates racism, healthcare racism etc. They the government provided you with socialism in a capitalist society, when you needed it. So why in the hell you think we don't need the same treatment! Therefore, the existing social services in the black communities are failing the people, because the governors know we will not survive without these agencies, and this is why DPS in this state of Michigan is trying to be phased out. This is a silent conspiracy by the governors to let our communities die out including the people. But they are steady making policies to help the immigrants and not the naturalize citizens and the Arabs and Jews are playing a big part in this tragedy! Negro's wake up!

Pray for America

Let us pray for America to become greater! The righteous will overcome this evilness!

Student loans

It is amazing how the capitalist brokers make money off students trying to go to college and loan out high interest loans, that will make learning higher education a struggle for the young. College should be free!

Dignity

Young black men, pull your pants up, have dignity with your struggles and God will prevail for you!

Greedy politicians

Politicians are becoming very greedy, and we must hold them accountable. Over 59 percent of black young men unemployed, this is wrong. A pipeline to prison and they know this!

Honor

Wake up young black men and women, honor is the key to your salvation!

Political chess

Let the games continue Trump=Lucifer, Sanders=Christ, Clinton=pawn place your chess pieces in order!

Marijuana Ordinance

The marijuana ordinance in the city of Detroit is a joke. Last night on fox 2 it was shown that all these dispensaries in my district was selling illegal drugs. Let's see how fast the mayor, city council and the chief of police attack this problem. The underhanded corruption is widespread reaching into our local government, such as Wayne County treasurer's office, Building and safety offices, and any office that allow these buildings to be occupied illegally! It's time for the people to march on City Hall and the dispensaries.

State surplus

You know how the local and state government in Michigan came up with a surplus. It's from the money that they are supposed to take care of the Black communities in this state.

Raggedy old houses

We have all these raggedy ass old houses in the black communities, because nobody's come up with a plan to renovate and modernize our communities, like they do in the white cities over America! Racism has set us so far back, and this is a disgrace to mankind!

Capitalism

Black people can no longer afford to live under a capitalist ideology! Vote for Bernie Sanders!

White people standup

White people stand up and obey thy God for the righteousness of his namesake, for you have made a mockery of his name!

Broken Covenant

The covenant of God is being broken so many, many times, you would think by now the humans would know and fear the wrath of God!

Immigration

The governors are slowly slipping in the immigrants from Syria and making our country unstable with fear and undermining our economy!

White Education

Why is it that with all the funds that spend for education in the white communities they are not faced with the school districts going broke, like in the Urban schools, and they always come up with someone mismanaging the funds. When they know damn well they didn't put the appropriate amount to be spend in the budget in the first place.

WE HOLD THESE TRUTHS

WE hold these truths to be self-evidence, that the secretary of state should declare white politicians to be perpetrators of genocide against black minorities in the United States of America, we can no longer depend on them to help us

communities out, because they are taking more pride in providing welfare and care for the immigrants that they are bringing into this country. So, the pot can't talk about the kettle! They have passed over our right for ethnic enclavement for years and are still doing it!

Jew is not a RACE

People being a Jew is not a race! It's a religion. Some white people want you to believe they have a favor in the Lord's eyes, but they don't! Donald Trump stated in his speech today his daughter was having a Jewish baby! How dumb can you get? That's not the baby's race. The so-called Jew's was from Germany and Russia and was given the state of Israel. The real Jew's are ones from Ethiopia and Africa! They were not Caucasian's! So, Mr. Trump and all you people get it straight!

White politicians

How can a white politician get up on stage and speak of issues, that is going to divide this country and not bring us the people together, because we are all GODs children. How can you open the door for immigrants and close the door on migrant Mexican workers? Is this a race issue. Since all the ones running came up under immigrant families who came to this country and enjoy the pleasures of ethnic enclavement. Why do they feel that black people don't have these same rights? We have helped the white people in this country fight in every war that they have started, and we still don't get any respect. But you can give more respect to the so call Jew in their welfare state in which we send our tax dollars to support and let them build their own nation. You brought the Arab over after destroying Iraq and let them become capitalist off the backs of black neighborhoods, now they own their own banks. You let the Russian quietly come in and gain businesses. Now you are sneaking in the Syrian immigrants who identify closely to your whiteness but are you making a serious mistake of letting the enemies in also! We need a politician to protect the country and unite all people for the betterment of social justice for all!

Michigan State Police (racial profiling)

You would think the Michigan state police would be under investigation, by the State Attorney General, the governor, the mayors and United States Justice Dept, due to one of their own kind has accused them of racial profiling and unequal employment opportunities for other ethnic races they service in the communities!

Allegiance

Politicians don't even believe in their allegiance to the flag or Americans. Their allegiance is to the big capitalist businesses and not the people!

Lottery

Good evening! Word for today. If the state's lottery commissioners did not get together to pick you a Powerball six-digit number, that's because they are not ready for anyone to win. They need the money to register really high so that the tax revenue can pay for whatever investment they have to pay off! Because the money sure isn't paying off the community debts! How selfish can these people be when the country is in deep debt! You know how many people that could be pulled up out of poverty. Probably giving the revenue to the Queen of England! Silly America

Relationships

Remember it takes two people to have a healthy relationship. If you find yourself always trying to force the other person to help and they always remain selfish and vain, then you need to remove this garbage out and get some new furniture in, or just be by your damn self! Start 2016 off by putting yourself first and cleaning house!

Religion

We place too much energy on defining one's religion instead of defining who we are and what is our purpose. There is no proof that your religions are connected to the Messiah!!!!!!!!!!!!!

Flint water crisis Lead

Flint Michigan should be declared a disaster area by President Obama at Gov. Rick Snyder request and a reparation bill should be underwritten by the federal government at the State's request. The damage has been done and everyone needs new housing at the governor's request!

Soulfulness

There is no soulfulness joy to "Rapping", we must start "Singing" again to communicate with our souls to bring unity and peace, within our communities! This is how the Whiteman is controlling the young black minds. The "Rapping" is stopping our communication with each other, but "Singing" brings out the soulfulness that the "Messiah" intended for us to keep us in unity with his spirit!

Classless

Blackman and black women don't allow yourselves to become classless, as to no longer see yourself in the mirror!

Socialization of the Blackman

BLACKMAN STAND UP AND SOCIALIZE AND DECRIMINALIZE YOURSELF FROM SELF HATRED, POVERTY, AND EDUCATE YOURSELF FROM THE ADDICTIONS THAT BRING YOU DOWN, IN ORDER TO LIFT YOURSELF UP!

Desocialization of Negro's in America

THE DESOCIALIZATION AND CRIMINALIZING OF NEGRO'S IN AMERICA AND AROUND THE WORLD HAS FINALLY CAME TO BARE FRUIT UPON OUR PEOPLE AND COMMUNITIES!

High morals Black women and Blackman

The Black woman's morals are very high, depending on the environment and family structure that she was raised under! White women let their white men rape and sexually harassed people of color for centuries! This is also true for black men, that's why the Whiteman terrorize us with poverty and separation of splitting up the family! But we are still morally strong!

Corrupted Lottery

The State Lottery Association is corrupted and cheating us all that play! They are cheating because they are allowed to use electronic drawings so that they can choose whatever numbers they draw to win, and they freeze out numbers that they don't want to win, and they place the winning numbers in stores that is in a highly white populated area. So we don't have a honest chance to win.

GUN CONTROL!!!!!!!!

WE NEED GUN CONTROL, YOU IDIOTS IN THE WHITEHOUSE, YOU SHOULD REALIZE THIS, TOO MANY MENTAL UNSTABLE PEOPLE WITH GUNS!THIS IS THE TERRORIST FROM WITHIN EACH COMMUNITY, CAN STRIKE ANYTIME!!!!!!IT IS OUT OF CONTROL!!!!!!

Negro's standup!!

ALL NEGRO'S IN AMERICA STAND UP AND BE COUNTED, BY DEVELOPING YOUR MIND, MORALS,HEALTH,WELFARE OF LIFE TO YOUR HIGHEST POTENTIALS OF HOW TO SURVIVE IN A WHITEMAN'S WORLD!!!!!!!LET'S FLIP THE SCRIPT!!!!!!

Charity all Year long

To the Celebrities and Politicians' people don't just need your charity on holidays, or turkey's and other things. We need your support all year long. We need for you to make the right decisions to help the poor all year long!

It's time to stop with being the ignorant black woman

It takes ignorant, stupid ass black females who don't how to appreciate a goodman but would rather let their feelings for that man corrupt the feelings of a child and his father! Are you this stupld, ass black female? Don't keep a good father from their children! Step up and be the woman GOD intended you to be for the sake of your children!

Urban Entitlements

Are the Urban cities receiving their entitlements from the federal government? Is the state and local government writing grants to get these entitlement grants from the federal level? The governor of this state of Michigan, made sure the skills and vocational trades were removed from the state's budget, even though the federal grants are available, and the Mayor of Detroit is not making sure we get our entitlements like all the white communities! The Blacks in America are just as American as all these white foreigners and they are also getting our entitlements from this racist government!

Outsourcing and Overpricing

THE POLITICIANS ARE BANKRUPTING AMERICANS WITH THIS HEALTHCARE AND AUTOMOBILE INSURANCES BOTTOM LINE!!!LET"S VOTE THEIR ASSES OUT!THESE POLITICIANS IS OUTSOURCING AND OVER PRICING OUR FUTURE!!!!!!!!!

Jesus the JEW?

Question? If Jesus was a Jew and the people that persecuted him was Jewish, then why are the Jews held in such high authority and receive modern day wealth, and social accommodations that Gentiles who live in poverty don't have. I feel something is wrong with this story!

A letter to Ben Carson

A letter to Ben Carson, secretary of H.U.D and Donald Trump, President. I know you righteous men care about the people in the Urban cities such a s Detroit, St, Louis, Selma, Compton and any other black city where people are hurting, because of poverty. So, I want to give you this message from the Messiah. Because of the high cost of mortgages, rent, healthcare, and auto insurance the poor people is not surviving. Here in Detroit, they build up the downtown areas, but forget about the neighborhoods. We have single parents, with young children and they need the entitlements that the government is supposed to offer to help them move up the ladder from poverty. So it was nice of you to visit Detroit, but you have made no plans to build more Section 8 apartments and you need to provide Section 235 homes, by contracting with building contractors to upgrade these old ageless houses, because you know the infrastructure is old and outdated causing lead and other bacteria to enter our drinking waters. The Messiah put you in a position to ring the bell of GLORY TO the Newborn KING!

False Allegiance

Certain leaders of this great Nation don't feel that Black people should not have a choice on standing to salute the flag of allegiance. Well, if you have been terrorized by poverty, racism, and your parental rights removed because you are unemployed and the police will kill you like its a sport. Most of the foster care system is composed of black children, now being put in white persons homes. You the American government want let us invest in our own neighbors, You disenfranchise us, remove all fathers from raising their children and put them in prisons. And its gotten to the point of our young men and women have no hope for the future. This is why we bow our heads and get on our knees in shame of the American flag and the government! Can I get a witness!

Smoking Weed

IS SMOKING WEED MAKING HUMANS IRRESPONSIBLE, WITH A JUST DON'T GIVE A DAMN ATTITUDE! ARE YOU A PART OF THE PROBLEM IN MAKING THESE HUMANS WEAK!

Help others

What are we doing to help others, stand up and be strong!

Part of the problem

ASK YOURSELF, AM I APART OF THE PROBLEM, OR APART OF THE ANSWER TO HELP MY BROTHERS AND SISTERS SURVIVE ON THIS PLANET!

GODLY

IF YOU ARE GODLY, YOU WILL NOT DO UNGODLY THINGS! THIS ATTITUDE WILL MAKE A BETTER WORLD FOR ALL OF US! GREAT THINGS WILL HAPPEN TO YOU!

China free healthcare

If CHINA can produce a universal healthcare reform for their people. Then what's wrong with all these idiot politicians in America. We need free universal healthcare. And all you middle class white people need to wake up, the government has free healthcare for their politicians, what's good for them should be better for the American people! Down with OBAMACARE and up with FREE UNIVERSAL HEALTHCARE! People can't pay their high mortgages with all these costly healthcare and auto insurance premiums. There is nothing wrong with a socialist ideology to help Americans. And doctors sure as hell not healing anyone, just giving them narcotics and you wonder why there is an opioid epidemic! Wake the hell up

Boycott Whitehouse

Let's boycott the Whitehouse, do you know that 99 percent of the customer services jobs are given to overseas because they can be hired for cheaper labor, just like the government sold out our manufacturing jobs to CHINA. The Whitehouse has sold out our country because they can no longer run this country on capitalism due to the high cost to manage wages and operational expenses, so they outsource our jobs. Silly white Americans wake up, it's not about race. It's about saving this country for all Americans regardless of the color of their skins! The solution is to transfer your ideology to democratic socialism, run by the people and for the good will of all mankind!

Americas in a crisis

This country is in a crisis, we are letting politicians program us to disaster, for their own selfish means. By proving for people indigent and showing the young black people in the Urban Cities that America still cares, then we can cut down on so much crime, that's sending our black young people to jail. We need a kinder, gentler nation to spring back into action. We need the politicians to take care of the people to pull us up and stop kicking us down! War is evil, poverty is evil, hatred is evil. This is not why God created this world, so why practice satanism!

American Dream Foreigners

WHY IS IT THE ARAB-CHALDEANS AND ASIAN INDIANS AND THE CHINESE ABLE TO COME IN AND OCCUPY ALL OUR BUSINESSES IN THE BLACK COMMUNITY, AND MARIJUANA SHOPS,BUT DON'T WANT TO PUT ANY OF

OUR MONIES BACK INTO OUR COMMUNITY!THIS IS A CONSPIRACY LEAD BY THE WHITE PEOPLE AND SOME BLACKS WHOM WE VOTED FOR!BEFORE VOTING FOR A NEW MAYOR OR COUNSELOR,,OR GOVERNOR,LET'S SEE HOW THEY CAN CORRECT THESE ISSUES,BEFORE ALLOWING THEM TO REPRESENT US THE COMMUNITY!I RECALL BACK IN THE DAY,WHEN WE VOTED FOR COLEMAN YOUNG,BUT IN HIS STRUGGLES,HE COMMITTED THE BIGGEST MISTAKE,WHEN HE GAVE THESE ARABS THE KEYS TO THE CITY,AND DID NOT REPRESENT OUR PEOPLE SO THAT THEY COULD KEEP THEIR BLACK BUSINESSES!HE LET US DOWN!SO IF HIS SON "COLEMAN YOUNG JR", WANTS TO BECOME MAYOR,HE BETTER RECOGNIZE,THAT THIS IS A BIG PROBLEM AND SET UP A STRATEGY TO GET THE BLACK COMMUNITY A BANK WHERE WE CAN GET MONIES SUCH AS THE ARABS,AND RUN THESE CAMEL JOCKEYS OUT OF THE MARIJUANA BUSINESS AND BEER AND WINE ON EVERY CORNER OF OUR BLACK NEIGHBORHOODS.WE DON'T NEED PROMISES WE NEED "ACTION"!YOU MUST BE A LEADER THAT PROVIDES FOR THE COMMUNITY AND NOT TAKE FROM THE COMMUNITY!THIS IS WHY WE HAVE SO MUCH CRIME AND THE YOUNG PEOPLE DON'T SEE ANY FUTURE FOR THEMSELVES SEEING ALL THESE FOREIGNERS ON EVERY CORNER OF OUR BLACK COMMUNITIES AND THEY DON'T GIVE A DAMN ABOUT BLACK PEOPLE!

Ungodly things

LET NO MAN OR WOMAN PUT IN MY MIND TO DO UNGODLY THINGS, FOR GOD IS OUR HOLY SAVIOR AND HE RULES WITH THE POWER OF RIGHTEOUSNESS!

God power

The power of GOD is within us all, use it for truth and goodness!

Economical bondage

Black people you are GODS, that's why we lack the spirit to kill. The white people are the Devil's people that's why they have the spirit to kill and destroy and to keep us in economical bondage!

Pipeline to Jail

NO HIGH SCHOOL DIPLOMA, NO GED CERTIFICATE IS A PIPELINE TO JAIL! THEY WILL LEAD YOU TO AN APPRENTICESHIP OR COLLEGE AND YOUR FIRST JOB!DON'T LET THESE WHITE CONSERVATIVES MAKE YOU A VICTIM OF THEIR GREED AND RACISM!

Trick or treat

They have all these new construction ventures coming to Detroit, but the Mayor nor the Governor has set up paid apprenticeship training jobs for the young black men and women in Detroit to be trained on, so that they could get jobs from the companies that get the contracts. And on top of that wants to close most of the Detroit Education system down. But I bet you they got the apprenticeship jobs in prison! I smell a government conspiracy and it's keeping black America down!

Weed

DO TO THE FAILURE OF THE LOCAL GOVERNMENT IN DETROIT TO MONITOR THESE MEDICAL MARIJUANNA SHOPS ON EIGHT MILE ROAD, ANOTHER GENERATION OF YOUNGBLACK PEOPLE WILL BE DESTROYED, BECAUSE

THEY ARE LETTING THE MEDICAL MARIJUANNA BEING ILLEGALLY SOLD ON THE STREETS.

Trumpism

Why is it that white people of America is letting Trump and the Politicians make a mockery out of what is good for the citizens in regards to healthcare premiums Who are they working for, because this is all about profit, and who receives it at the top. Are the politicians working for the insurance industry, because they certainly are not working for the citizens of America? And Trump is acting like a bully leading a gang of thugs, and you people is satisfied with this! He is not working for the citizens. He is overturning whatever OBAMA has done because he is jealous and a racist!

Capitalism

Capitalism is killing poor people and is now reaching for the middle class! We will become a MAD MAX society soon, if we don't dump these crazy selfish politicians!

Protect and Serve

It is a shame how the white policemen who are hired to protect and serve, easily pull out their gun and shoot you because you are of a different color. Is it not true that they are hired to protect and serve all people regardless of their established racist ideology! And if they can't do this they need to get another job!

Insurance corruption

Politicians are using healthcare premiums and automobile insurance as a means to pull over 55 percent of your income from your paychecks, besides taxes so you want to have any money to save or spend for your future and your children's future!

Richer or Poorer

It is time for Americans to start loving and caring about one another. The children, the poor need politicians that care about the poor, and care about becoming a kinder, gentler nation that will promote the wellbeing of the nation, so that we can express and feel love for one another! A cap must be put on the profit margin of Capitalism, because it has destroyed the growth of the cities and communities of the people that helped build this great country, at the expense of making the wealthy, richer!

America's Arab, Indian, Chinese businesses in the Black communities

WHY IS IT THE ARAB-CHALDEANS AND ASIAN INDIANS AND THE CHINESE ABLE TO COME IN AND OCCUPY ALL OUR BUSINESSES IN THE BLACK COMMUNITY, AND MARIJUANA SHOPS,BUT DON'T WANT TO PUT ANY OF OUR MONIES BACK INTO OUR COMMUNITY!THIS IS A CONSPIRACY LEAD BY THE WHITE PEOPLE AND SOME BLACKS WHOM WE VOTED FOR!BEFORE VOTING FOR A NEW MAYOR OR COUNSELOR,,OR GOVERNOR,LET'S SEE HOW THEY CAN CORRECT THESE ISSUES,BEFORE ALLOWING THEM TO REPRESENT US THE COMMUNITY!I RECALL BACK IN THE DAY,WHEN WE VOTED FOR COLEMAN YOUNG,BUT IN HIS STRUGGLES,HE

COMMITTED THE BIGGEST MISTAKE,WHEN HE GAVE THESE ARABS THE KEYS TO THE CITY,AND DID NOT REPRESENT OUR PEOPLE SO THAT THEY COULD KEEP THEIR BLACK BUSINESSES!HE LET US DOWN!SO IF HIS SON "COLEMAN YOUNG JR", WANTS TO BECOME MAYOR,HE BETTER RECOGNIZE,THAT THIS IS A BIG PROBLEM AND SET UP A STRATEGY TO GET THE BLACK COMMUNITY A BANK WHERE WE CAN GET MONIES SUCH AS THE ARABS,AND RUN THESE CAMEL JOCKEYS OUT OF THE MARIJUANA BUSINESS AND BEER AND WINE ON EVERY CORNER OF OUR

BLACK NEIGHBORHOODS.WE DON'T NEED PROMISES WE NEED "ACTION"!YOU MUST BE A LEADER THAT PROVIDES FOR THE COMMUNITY AND NOT TAKE FROM THE COMMUNITY!THIS IS WHY WE HAVE SO MUCH CRIME AND THE YOUNG PEOPLE DON'T SEE ANY FUTURE FOR THEMSELVES SEEING ALL THESE FOREIGNERS ON EVERY CORNER OF OUR BLACK COMMUNITIES AND THEY DON'T GIVE A DAMN ABOUT BLACK PEOPLE!

Diana Ross

It's amazing I went to school with Diana Ross, Bishop elementary and I watched her sing at the Ebenezer Baptist church right off Canfield and Alexandrine. I also lived across the street from Berry Gordy's brother, and he used to come into our apt building 300 Canfield, those was the precious days right down the street from the Flame show bar and the Graystone ballroom, and the Madison ballroom by the Vernor's pop company on Woodward Ave. Detroit MI. Days to remember!

Moral responsibility

Youngman and Young women, it is your moral duty to rise above those that bring you down by Lust and pain that they are having and want to inflict you with this disease of not making the distinction between right and wrong. Don't let sinful people hi-jack your love for yourself and discipline yourself to make choices of what is right from what is wrong!

Healthcare wall street commodity

The politicians have made healthcare a commodity for wall street and more expensive than saving lives! Traders and cowards running the government and none of them have balls enough to stand up for the people who put them in office!

Mandatory healthcare

Mandatory Healthcare is the worst mandate that the government has placed on Americans. Especially on those who are economically hurting!

Corrupt credit score agencies

WHY IS IT WE LET THIS GOVERNMENT GET AWAY WITH ALLOWING CREDIT SCORES TO BE APART OF DETERMINING HOW WE CAN GET INSURANCE FOR OUR CARS, HOMES, LIFE INSURANCE, THESE THINGS ARE APART OF OUR NECESSITIES.NOW IF THEY PREFER TO USE THIS FOR CREDIT CARDS,THAT'S DIFFERENT,BECAUSE WE ACTUALLY DON'T NEED THESE CREDIT CARDS!AND ALSO THEY USE THESE SCORES TO DISCRIMINATE WITH ALSO!

Middle Class

MIDDLECLASS AMERICANS ARE ONLY WORKING FOR THE BIG TIME GOVERNMENT CEO'S, MAKING PAYMENTS ON

HIGH INTEREST RATE LOANS, HEALTHCARE,HIGH AUTO INS,AND MORTGAGES.AND THE POOR PEOPLE ARE NOT MAKING IT AT ALL!

America's Enslavement

OTHER THAN BEING ENSLAVED BY RACISM IN AMERICA.NOW THE POLITICIANS HAVE FOUND A NEW WAY TO ENSLAVE US ALL, THROUGH HEALTHCARE, AUTO INSURANCE, HOMEOWNERS INS, LIFE INS, HIGH INTEREST RATES, CREDIT SCORING AND ECONOMICAL OPPRESSION!THIS HAS BECOME AN AMERICAN NIGHTMARE RATHER THAN AN AMERICAN DREAM!

Good morning

GOOD MORNING, BEAUTIFUL PEOPLE, I WANT YOU TO HAVE A GREAT, SAFE, BEAUTIFUL DAY AND BE THANKFUL AND BLESSED!

Obamacare

The only reason the Republicans rush to repeal Obamacare is because this was a Blackman who introduced the bill, and Trump went alone with this stupidity. Known of them has the best interest of the citizens and it's all about who can make the most profit. And we just sit and go along with whatever! I need free healthcare, and until they explain to me why there is a deductible with three digits, they can go to HELL!

Get thee behind me

BLACKPEOPLE IN AMERICA, WITHOUT A WAR CHEST OF MONEY WE HAVE NO FUTURE.GET THEE BEHIND ME AND I WILL CHALLENGE THE CONSTITUTION AND EXISTENCE OF EVERY URBAN CITY IN AMERICA.

Rapping is Poison

Sermon for today! To all the rappers out there, you have failed your people, because the Whiteman that sponsored you knew that this rap would make the Blackman more competitive with each other and would only further segregate us from each other. Just like having a rapping contest is like being in the boxing ring, trying to knock each other out spiritually and mentally. It removes the love that we are supposed to have for each other. Instead, it makes us war against each other. That is why the white Jewish producers such as SONY and others back you guys. They have shut down the singing of rhythm and blues, and jazz, because it captures our soulfulness and spirit to love one another. That is why we are having so much crime in the hood, because you are making our young black men and women practice war within their souls, because they feel the pain of being disenfranchised in this Whiteman's world and no one is doing anything about it.

Don't Rock the Boat "OBAMA

All your black people praising Obama, show me one thing he did to help the Blackman, he played it safe and did not rock the Whiteman's agenda of making the murder rates in the black community go up and not down, by not providing mandatory technical courses in the high schools, so that these young black students could at least learn an apprentice job so they could get work after high schools. He allowed people like Gov. Snyder to break the education system in Detroit by crippling and closing schools to force a college prep on the kids knowing they were not prepared for it, and just crippled special education!

Where's the POPE

Where is the POPE, and religious leaders, don't they see that America has become ethically and morally corrupt with all these online instant videos, and the news media and Hollywood and rap. Desensitizing the cruelty and criminal acts that are playing our country. This must stop someone has to form a new committee to put regulations on censoring cellphone cameras. What being shown on television and what the news media can show.

Hidden Figures

Its amazing how the Whiteman try to keep the Negro's history hidden. As in the movie "Hidden Figures" in which some Negro woman were brilliant mathematicians and they have never mention one word about this in the schoolbooks, nor the news media back in the day. I wonder how many more surprises will come available for Negro people to learn about! That's why they don't have a academic course for Negro History in the schools. This should be against the civil rights law!

Republican Conspiracy: The WALL

The Democrats are not the problem, it's those crazy Racist Republicans. A wall is needed to keep out all the persons of color. But with the situation of all the marijuana being made legal in America, which means if there is a call for more military assistance, then most of the male and female population will be suffering from some type of recreational drug abuse and can't enlist for services. Now there's where the Republican conspiracy comes in and will help Russia or China if they ever want to start war. We will have closed off the border and all those future young people want be able to enlist and help us protect our country, thanks to Trump!

Adoption of black children by Whites is wrong

The children rights advocacy association should be ashamed at letting black children be adopted by the poor whites and the wealthy movie stars, example "Charlize Theron from south Africa is the prime reason an investigation needs to be started in how she is raising those black children is crazy and abusive. If this was a black person, it would be all over the news.

It is Written

You know they say there is a curse on the black race, (slavery and poverty and imprisonment). But the master wants me to enlighten you, there is also a curse on the so-called white people (privileged, wealth, racism and killing). Their young will devour them with mass killings. They are the killing machines of the earth. Therefore, we have WAR for no reason! Therefore, they get a lesser sentence for a crime, because they must get out and commit more of these insane acts! Blacks kill out of frustration bought on by the racist system (still no excuse), but white's kill just out of having to

much of a good thing and wanting more! They are also changing the master's creation of what gender should be male or female! It is written!

Down with the two-party systems

In my time of thought. The master wants me to enlighten you about politics. Why do we need a two-party system? They only fight amongst each other in a power struggle for the rich! WE need a one-party system for the people and by the people! One parliament of humans to make sure the leader, the President works for the commonwealth of the people who put him into power! Get rid of the two-party system!!!!!!!!

Politicians or Murders

Why is it we go to war, such as what is happening over in Yemen, or any other country to kill the people over oil, or land that is rightfully the ownership of the people that reside there! The problem is we have been allowing this to go on for too long! Look at Libya, there was no reason to go into that country and kill their leader Ghaddafi, and now they sell people into slavery. Thanks to the past President Obama, and now look at what is happening to the new President Trump, Lier, Lier! Can we entrust our Presidents to promote peace around the world?

Democrats and Republicans Enemies of the People

A word to the wise. Democrats and Republicans are not working for the poor nor middle class anymore. They insist upon making the white middle class think that Blacks are taking their freedoms, and throw racism at the doorsteps of the whitepapers they can become consumed with hatred for their brothermen....They lobby for the wealthy and not the poor nor middleclass. They take most of your hard-earned dollars, at least 89 percent to give to the CEO's and the wealthy, and then make you feel that it's the black people that are making life hard for them in America! And satisfy the CEO's and wealthy with keeping healthcare, auto insurance, mortgage rates, and prices are at the top of the ceiling. So you white people, middle class people need to no, you are being played. But this also hurt the poor and you never will be able to get up out of poverty! White America wakes the hell up, it is not about "Hatred or Racism "it's about all for one and one for all. The world is big enough for all of us. And the police need to wake the hell up also and stop venting their post-traumatic stress out on Black people, we are not the cause of this country's problems. WAKEUP

Fake Lottery System

If this was a true lottery, they would not have let one person win 1.6 billion dollars. Instead it should have been 1 million to a million Americans, instead of the Lottery Association getting most of the money for tax revenue to divide up in each state. And there is no proof what they use it for!

Political Mess

What kind of political system is in place when the people we elect go into their jobs and have a pension, better healthcare and a very good salary, that we pay for, and they vote against pensions, good healthcare and cheaper auto insurance. They don't service the community who placed them into their good paying political jobs. Something is wrong with this process!

Imperialism vs Capitalism

We are living in a very trying time. Our politicians, democrats and republicans have been swayed into being more of an Imperialist ideology, rather than a true democratic capitalist society! And this means both parties.! And you can take this to the bank, if we don't pull up out of it we will be destroyed by these Imperialist pigs controlling our government! Race isn't got nothing to do with it!

ADVOCATE FOR POVERTY

You can't be an advocate for the poor, if you don't add a little socialist idea into the democratic process of truly resolving the problems that this capitalist system has damaged. Capitalism carries many different bias, such as unequal distribution of wealth, racism, and unequal justice for all. If one pledges allegiance to their country. Then why should one not want to except free healthcare, free education, lower interest rates etc.? Capitalism has overflowed its meaning of democracy and must be capped with socialism, or the people will die a slow death of being in poverty and there will be no middle class!

Social Services blackout

On Fox2 channel this morning they showed a black man and his child living in a tent! There are a lot of Black families and young people living in the streets. My question is. If Fox2 and other news media get involved with the war on poverty in the black communities, we could put pressure on the Governor and Mayor to make Michigan State Dept of Human Services step up and start helping the black communities in this state! They cut food stamps and Medicaid knowing damn well people are hurting more than ever. I know because I see this happening in my community. Poverty is just a silent terrorist, and it destroys poor communities and Detroit, Flint, Ypsilanti, and other major black cities are under attack. You know why because social services have refused to provide for the poor, they failed their mission, because some leader got the bright idea to cut back monies that the Federal government gives them to run the cities in this state. Why am I voting if my voice is not being heard. I know the tricks of government and it is to make the middleclass think they are middleclass, but they just as poor as the poor. Social services depend on the black eligibility workers to deny their people, and not have empathy and compassion for their own community and it works. The old people die, and the young ones survive by doing CRIME! Get up off your degreed asses and help your

PEOPLE! News media start interviewing the directors and find out what are they doing for the poor. Put them on the spot!

Difference between democrats/republicans

What's the difference between a Democrat and Republican? The way I look at it. The Democrats at least make you think they are the grass roots of liberty, justice, and social wellbeing of your existence, and they try not to let big business dictate to them on how to run the government. The Republicans try to make the middle class feel that they have all the good morals, and keep taxes at a low level, but they are in big businesses pockets, and this is what keeps the wealthy, wealthy. They sneak back in the middle-class door and have high interest rates for the banks and raise the prices on the things like medical insurance, mortgages, food prices, gas prices, high auto insurance rates. This affects about 85 percent of your household income. Then they make you feel that the poor is the cause for all these problems. You don't need a degree to see what's going on. So they cut food stamps, cut Medicaid, cut anything that will help your kids and mine to get up off the ground. And this is why we have a lot of Millennials still at home or coming back. This is no way to run a country. You give Social Services so those people can get trainings and jobs, so the middle class can continue to grow! Stop worrying about who's getting free food, or free medical, none of us was born with a silver spoon in our mouths. Remember do unto others as you would want them to do unto you! Get some common sense!

MDHHS Mission

You know the attack on poverty in this state of Michigan is sad. MDHHS mission is supposed to help lift people out of poverty, and this cannot be done with people putting their nose up in the air. The Governor, Mayor, President and politicians and Social Workers knows damn well that cutting food stamps and Medicaid benefits is going to cause hardships on our people! You go to college and get your degrees just to make a large paycheck, but you are lacking in the humanitarian efforts of helping people move up the ladder to get middle class status. In this city there is no accountability for workers not answering their phones and the Governor and Mayor don't give a shit, whether the workers serve their customers with dignity and respect. Why is social services in business if they are not serving the blacks in their communities? I say this because the white counties serve their people with respect, but our black eligibility workers with their 2 years of college don't represent our black community with passion nor empathy, nor dignity and respect, because the white leaders at the top Director of Social services want it this way in the black communities, and this will criminalize our people into doing harm to one another. They would rather deny you benefits than approve them. Wayne County Social Services does not serve the people in our communities.

Diversify the Supreme Court Justice

You know I find something wrong in how the constitution made the plan for how you choose the Supreme Court Justice, it should be updated. America is a nation of diverse people, and the Court should represent this. There should be a Senate or Congress reviewing this unequal situation of having one in authority to choose who sits on the bench. America is very diverse in its races, such as the people that is on the bench should represent White America, Black America, Asian America, Indian American, and Multiracial Americans. Also, there should be 5 females and 4 males. Because the white male is the majority, that is why I say 4 males of different races.

Justice

It is of distaste that I see the nominee chosen for the Supreme Court Justice have a complete emotional breakdown, when he is supposed to represent being fair and equal to all mankind! If we get upset over a black person kneeling Pledging the Allegiance, why should not we get upset when you turn your backs on a female stating "I was sexually harassed by that man? If the nominee shows any weakness and emotions. He should remove himself from the process! Does not this Pledge, state Justice for All?

Malcolm X Chickens comes home to Roost

Well as "Malcolm X" stated the "Chickens are coming home to ROOST", it seems like the Whiteman has built this country up on sexually abusing females, black women and white women, and even men, due to the privilege of putting themselves above the law and the unequal justice that is imposed on people of color. It is very clear that his own white female is going to put a rope around his own neck!

KNEELING BEFORE THE PLEDGE

Since when we the people let the government tell us when to pray and when not to kneel! God's law is much greater, and we must not allow ourselves to be covenant by the devil's disciples. If you let other people and these nuts in government offices tell you not to pray or when to kneel. Then you are not a warrior for GOD! The federal, state and local government needs GOD and shall not separate any state, federal, and local matters without prayer or kneeling! War does not make hero's; it makes killers out of men! Then you wonder why they come home suffering from PSTD Fighting wars for the democrats and republicans, does not make heroes, but fools of us all. So, stop thinking kneeling is a crime or a smack in the face to the military it's not. It's a salute to GOD, letting the creator know, we are in trouble down here and we need the country (Flag) to come together, and there is no justice under this flag for people of color!

PTSD

Most Whiteman suffer post-traumatic stress from war, and black men suffer post-traumatic stress from racism and the war. So, America needs to hurry up and change its ideology to a social revolution to ease the pain of both, racism and war. It's called the new democracy=democratic socialism=No more high auto insurance, no more high interest rates, the real universal healthcare, which is free healthcare, down with the corporations living off the poor and the middle class. If this does not happen, there will be no middle class and we will all be poor!

LOVE

Remember, LOVE is like a Melody, it comes from the heart!

LIFE

Don't let life take advantage of you, you take advantage of life!

Drugs Destroy

Drugs is just a bandage, don't get caught up, it will kill you or still make you a slay, and that's what the Whiteman wants. Be a warrior for who you are and don't let anyone tell you, that you are nothing, because you are somebody, you are Gods creation! Be very proud of that!

Pledge of Allegiance

As I see it in America, the white people are not honoring the "Pledge of Allegiance", because professionals like white policeman and white military, and white people in general are using "Racism "and "Hatred", to destroy this country. They don't understand that this pledge states {I} pledge everyone to justice for all., and they are not living up to their own pledge. All these senseless killings by white police are putting our country into disgrace and their superiors only have themselves to blame, instead of standing up and saying enough is enough, cause if you don't you will become a victim of your own creation!!!They become monsters above the law!

Military Upset WHY?

All this upset over "The pledge of allegiance to the flag, has nothing to do with the military, just because the President stated it was an insult to the military. He was side tracking just to not make himself look silly. And as usual the white military men took offense. This kneeling by black football players is a peaceful protest under the flag letting this American flag (of course not human),no that whatever it stands for we are not being representative as a race of people who have died and fought for this country under the same banner the Whiteman has died and fought for this country, and they enjoy the freedoms which, we the black people are being abused by white policemen who does not hold the same allegiance that the flag represents for all mankind. So you military people need to chill out and stop taking a stand against us kneeling in silence, because you are letting that idiot in the White House include you into his racism, so read the Allegiance which was created and written by a socialist minister Francis Bellamy. Let these truths be known to all men and women!

Pledge of Allegiance (Quote)

The Pledge of Allegiance

The Pledge of Allegiance was written in August 1892 by the socialist minister Francis Bellamy (1855-1931). It was originally published in The Youth's Companion on September 8, 1892. Bellamy had hoped that the pledge would be used by citizens in any country.

In its original form it read:

"I pledge allegiance to my Flag and the Republic for which it stands, one nation, indivisible, with liberty and justice for all."

In 1923, the words, "the Flag of the United States of America" were added. At this time it read:

"I pledge allegiance to the Flag of the United States of America and to the Republic for which it stands, one nation, indivisible, with liberty and justice for all."

in 1954, in response to the Communist threat of the times, President Eisenhower encouraged Congress to add the words "under God," creating the 31-word pledge we say today. Bellamy's daughter objected to this alteration. Today it reads:

"I pledge allegiance to the flag of the United States of America, and to the republic for which it stands, one nation under God, indivisible, with liberty and justice for all."

Section 4 of the Flag Code states:

The Pledge of Allegiance to the Flag: "I pledge allegiance to the Flag of the United States of America, and to the Republic for which it stands, one Nation under God, indivisible, with liberty and justice for all.", should be rendered by standing at attention facing the flag with the right hand over the heart. When not in uniform men should remove any non-religious headdress with their right hand and hold it at the left shoulder, the hand being over the heart. Persons in uniform should remain silent, face the flag, and render the military salute."

The original Bellamy salute, first described in 1892 by Francis Bellamy, who authored the original Pledge, began with a military salute, and after reciting the words "to the flag," the arm was extended toward the flag.'

At a signal from the principal the pupils, in ordered ranks, hands to the side, face the Flag. Another signal is given; every pupil gives the flag the military salute — right hand lifted, palm downward, to a line with the forehead and close to it. Standing thus, all repeat together, slowly, "I pledge allegiance to my Flag and the Republic for which it stands; one Nation indivisible, with

Liberty and Justice for all." At the words, "to my Flag," the right hand is extended gracefully, palm upward, toward the Flag, and remains in this gesture till the end of the affirmation; whereupon all hands immediately drop to the side.

Melody

My Melody, you have weathered the storm of life, and have had compassion, empathy and grace in raising your children, and a loving heart big enough to share in raising other people's children. Now it's time to relax and condition your own spirit, and enjoy your son, daughter, and grandchildren. Enjoy a healthy and wealthy gift of life yourself!

Crystal

Crystal, I want the world to know, you are a proud black female, who is a single parent, intelligent, has morals, not self-centered, has compassion, and empathy for others and loves her family and children. I salute you and thank you for being THAT KIND OF WOMAN!!!!!!We love you!!!!

Political Cowards

I feel all the politicians are two faced, and cowards for the sake of their own greed! They don't care anything about the people of the United States of America!

Negro Morals

We the Negro communities have got to get back into teaching the correct morals to our children, and don't let others change our values. Help save the current and future generations for our children's safe!

Political Cowards

I feel all the politicians are two faced, and cowards for the sake of their own greed! They don't care anything about the people of the United States of America!

NEGRO MORALS

We the Negro communities have got to get back into teaching the correct morals to our children, and don't let others change our values. Help save the current and future generations for our children's safe!

We need a Hero

There is a black holocaust going on in America and around the world. To many black men in prison, poverty, and crime! We need a Whiteman to stand up and bring this holocaust to an end! Poverty and racism make prisoners of us all! We were lucky in the 20 centuries to have a Blackman as president, but to no prevail, he did not one thing to help us to reverse some of the unrighteousness that was being done to our people. Then we get a full pledge white president that still is setting us back further and further with his ignorance. I have to say it but we the black people in America needs a white intelligent leader, that can pull us up out of bondage, because the black man has been brainwashed mentally that he is the problem in this world, he can't mentally stand up to these white racists, but another Whiteman can! We got to stop this poverty and racism! We need a HERO, not a pretty boy nor maniac in the White House!!!!!!!!

Confessions

Have you ever wondered, what the words, "bless me father I have sinned ", meant when a person is confessing to his priest. Could it be he's asking Lucifer instead of GOD to praise him for that sin?

Down with Democrats Republicans

The Democrats and the Republicans have fucked up America! It is time for a new day democracy to be built, we must confront all this greed and hatred with a new democracy for all the people. This democracy will be called "Socialist Democrat", it will stand for, all for one and one for all, for the people and by the people! If this does not happen in the next election, America will become a third world country. Blacks are already living in third world conditions in America!

Thou shall not KILL

Question? If you are a cop and kill someone, do you think GOD will forgive you? Question if you are a person and kill someone, do you think GOD will forgive you? If you are a soldier and kill someone, do you think GOD will forgive you? THOU SHALT NOT KILL!!

Florence

Florence was my beautiful mother, whom I miss every day of my life. She was my best friend, my confidante, my mom, my everything! She taught me to how to grow up and respect people, especially my elders! She loved and adored her family. In Winston-Salem N.C. we use to go into the restaurants and then into movies every weekend, she worked as a domestic in white people's homes, but she was a very proud "Negro

Woman", my father was bi-racial as this America determines the labeling of people of color. Eventually I became grown and started to have children and she taught me how to take care of each one of my babies, it was not my husband who taught me about our children, it was my MOM, whom I will love forever and ever and ever. Love you MOM, wherever your soul resides in the Universe!!She had so much LOVE and we were poor, but she kept food and clothes on my back regardless of her circumstances! It was hard for a "Negro woman "back in the day! But they were very, very strong Women of color, I salute them and give them the highest AWARD of being a caring human Mother!

Justice is dead

Is Justice in America dead? There are a lot of people thrown in prison that have mental health issues, after ENGLER closed all the mental health hospitals. This is a big issue, particularly on the increase of crime in the communities! Politicians are doing nothing about it.

Racism/Poverty

WHITE America is using RACISM and POVERTY to terrorize people of color!!!!!While they enjoy the best of everything!

Lawless

The federal government is no longer a democracy, because the politicians have made it a private political entity that profits for themselves and to hell with the patriotism this country was built on! The states have become a political private entity also, and they allow our protectors (white Policeman)to become lawless!

Child support

Young Ladies, do you know that if you have never been on welfare and your child's father gets behind in child support, you have the right to waive the support so that the child's father wants to go to jail. This is a state law! Stand up and take care of your child, don't let your children see that you will send their fathers to jail, give these guys some empathy! It is just as much as your responsibility to provide for your child if the man is unable too!

Humans

Are there any "HUMANS" existing in this Paranoid Schizophrenia world of today! And the main persons are our leaders! Come on people straighten up, we are in trouble with GOD!!!

Drugs

To tell the truth, the middle class started growing in 1950, when everyone was leaving the South to work at the automobile factories, as the blacks started merging into the middle-class economy, and this included the poor whites. But then the white politicians saw that we were winning the battle on integration and equality, they started dropping big loads of drugs in our communities. Don't the modern-day Whiteman realize that drugs have no name or color! And with the way the white politicians have sold our liberty to other nations, we will all be poor! Greed has corrupted this whole nation!

America legalized Sodomy

Most young people in America don't even realize the part they are playing when they become GAY. The realization of it all is they are committing one of the oldest crimes of mankind, Sodomy. Why America is going along with these gay people yelling for their human rights are being violated, I just don't know. Have not they ever read the bible or the ten commandments? Have they never heard or read the story about, "Sodom and Gomorrah". How God turned humans to stone. This is the nastiest of all sexual crimes. I have nothing against being a human, but to divert yourself into liking one of the same sexes is not normal. You are sodomizing each other which is a sin. There is also a concern about the government allowing these people to adopt and foster children. Humans wake up, you will be punish!

Diversity

Diversity is not about Gay people, it's about human rights and not about lusting rights!

Confessions

Have you ever wondered, what the words, "bless me father I have sinned, meant when a person is confessing to his priest? Could it be he asking Lucifer instead of GOD to praise him for that sin?

DOWN with the Democrats, Republicans

The Democrats and the Republicans have fucked Socialist Democrat", it will stand for, all for one and one for all, for the people and by the people! If this does not happen in the next election, America will become a third world country. Blacks are already living in third world conditions in America!

Babylon in America

Believe it or not, America has become the Babylon of the past. We are repeating the same sins that they practiced back then, and we will be punished by the Creator for these sins! Wake up before it is too late people!

White vs Black

Whiteman don't you understand to live in this world you cheated by making yourselves a majority and persons of color a minority, and then you want us to respect all the rules you make to keep yourselves on the top! Now you breath, sleep, die, get sick, catch the same bacteria's we catch, so how does that make you feel more superior to black people. Whiteman you need to wake the hell up and send racism packing, it will destroy the whole world! You make it easier for your own kind, so that you want make war (civil war) on each other, so that you can live in peace with each other, but you keep blacks at each other throats with poverty and prison, and removing the father from their families, while you make sure you are with yours. Look in the mirror and remove that demon DNA from your souls! Men

4th of July

July 4th means to me that there should have never been racism, wars or poverty in a country that is supposed to be one of the greatest melting pots of every country in this world! War does not make men, it destroys them! The victim's are the ones that had to die!!!!!

Government corruption

I truly don't believe any of our heads of states and cities, and the federal government swears allegiance to the flag, communities or our country anymore. They are full of greed and contempt and use us as pawns in a society full of hatred and crime and poverty! No one talks about the real issues of our manufacturing jobs in CHINA, foreigners owning our banks, automobile companies run by foreigners and greedy auto insurance companies, greedy healthcare providers.

AWAKE

Let's reach down deep into our souls and pull the real life to be lived out and stop all this foolishness of addictions we don't need! Stand up and live to love living! We only got one chance!

Sin

Do you know when its time to stop sinning, so that you can morally raise your children, who need you?

Love thyself

Learn to love oneself as if one is a King or Queen! There is no love amongst sinners, nothing but greed and selfishness!

Christian values

The Christian values that are being taught in church are not strong enough to help save the world!!!Because we reward ourselves with repenting over and repeatedly!!

No mass transportation

It is amazing that the legislatures rather allow "Uber" or "Lyft" transportation to service people that don't have cars, that need to get to their jobs in other countries or around the city, costing people big bucks. When all they need to do is sat money aside for "Mass Transit", which would be heaven sent to help people get from place to place in this stressful time of high cost of living. Just does not make sense in the 21st Century!!!

REVIEW CROSS RACIAL FOSTERING/ADOPTION

ALL STATES IN AMERICA SHOULD REVIEW THEIR POLICIES ON BLACKCHILDREN BEING ADOPTED TO SAME SEX PARENTS, AND PLACED IN WHITE PERSONS HOMES, FOR THE BEST INTEREST AND SAFETY OF BLACKCHILDREN ALL OVER THE WORLD!

Don't Apologize

White people, we as black people in America, don't want your "Apology" we just want "Equality"," Justice"., and "Freedom" to live in this world like you make yourselves privilege to live in this world, without "Racism"!

Generation of being privilege/Whiteman

It's very evident as I sat and watch D.Phil.., that the Whiteman's generation of being privilege in America, has caused a fallout of spoil brats that end up going to schools and committing mass murder. It is also evident as the black man lives in a world of racism and bigotry, our black children are having Post traumatic stress which causes them to do senseless crimes to one another and end up dead or in prison. America needs some true leadership to bring this country together! Racist white people have weakened the fabric of our country!

Legislate Justice for All

IT'S a shame how the majority of white police treat Black Americans. We need to legislate new laws to help protect the citizens' rights, when it comes to police brutality in America. If we can't trust most white policemen, then whom do we put our trust in. Is the pursuit of liberty dead! Are we in the wild, wild, west? NO! We are in a country that must protect our citizens, or justice is dead!!!!!!!!We need to provide for state and Federal laws to make the white police force, equal with Black police officers, so that they can be taught diversity in numbers! And what in the hell is the NAACP advocating for and the URBAN League? We need to march on the state's legislators and Washington D.C. its very obviously the state's representative has violated our civil rights, by allowing these states to hire a bunch of white racist policemen.

White people and hatred

White people need to once and for all get rid of their hatred for persons of color, can't they see how their hatred is driving their young to kill their own kind! This is not a mystery but should be studied! Give life to loving one another!

GOD'S MANY NAMES

THEY PREACH UPON THE NAME OF JESUS, BUT I HAVE MANY NAMES, AND NO ONE HAS EVER SEEM MY FACE! BUT BELIEVE IN THE WORD AND THE HOLY SPIRIT THAT I BRING TO YOU, FOR I AM THE FATHER AND THE SON. I AM ONE!

Under Siege in America

Black men and Black women, we are under siege by the white power structure in America, the handwriting is on the wall. Whether rich or poor. You are allowing your morals to become flawed and not living with the higher conscience of your Creator! We are letting the Whiteman destroy us! We are powerless and without financial backing in the United States of America!

Poverty

You can't have poverty in a country that practices "Capitalism". But it can be practiced in a "Socialist" country!

Crime

The government must provide for the poor, until they reach middle class status, because this will decrease crime in the neighborhoods for the safety of all!

New World Order

Have you looked at the cost of insurances lately, healthcare, homeowners, auto insurance, is this the way the NEW WORLD ORDER of politics is operating? Because the politicians don't care at all about the high cost of these items, that will eventually bankrupt every family in the United States. Someone in government is masterminding the cost while letting the government just overlook the price controls. Also, this is happening with prescription drugs also, but none of the politicians are interested in what is going on because they are getting kickbacks from the corporations.

Free healthcare and free education

Do you Americans realize that all the U.K. and other countries have free education and healthcare, and the silly American government makes you feel like this nation is not good enough to give these dedicated servicemen and women, and the people of America free healthcare and free education, don't you feel we have earned this for our patriotism!

Self Esteem

Young men and young women remember this old saying, if you lay down with a dog, you going to get up with fleas. Upgrade your self-esteem and be proud of yourself, so that you can raise your children to be proud of themselves and you!

The WORD

It's really nothing with living, walking, and talking with the word of GOD, try it you might just like it!

Wages of Sinning

Question? Do you feel that when you are sinning continuously, and know it, that there are no consequences? Those pleasures that you are seeking has just been loaned to you by the Devil, and when he wants payment, can you fulfill this debt with your life? But GOD will reward you for being obedient to his laws with the breath of life!

Self-Supporting

IT'S NOTHING WRONG WITH HELPING OUT THE POOR, SO THAT THEY CAN RISE UP AND HELP THEMSELVES BECOME SELF SUPPORTING!

False Christians

False Christians, if you want to dwell in the house of God. You must build his temple within your body and mind and soul!

Ridiculous USDA American Harvest Box

I just don't understand this "USDA American Harvest box" over $90 worth of cash for food stamps is "RIDICULOUS", we are not immigrants nor refugees. I would think the President to have empathy for the poor, and not grudge them out of what little bit, they get as American citizens. We the people can't help causing you stupid politicians send all our jobs overseas. No, the problem is that they open up the doors for the immigrants and this is costing to much for them to provide for us and the foreigners we did not tell them to overload the system with immigrants, they made these laws. So don't punish the American citizens just because you stupid politicians can't balance the funking budget! American people stand up for your rights, or we will be running a "MAD MAX SOCIETY". Do you hear me?

FDA/PRESCRIPTION DRUGS CORRUPTION

Prescription drug costs are corrupted in these United States of America and we are not during or saying one thing about it! The FDA should be ashamed of themselves and the politicians!

Difference between ground and surface water(Quote)

Detroit is receiving surface water, Flint receives surface water, Ecorse receives surface water, and most other white cities receive ground waters, so what's the difference.
BACKGROUND: Every day, the average American uses about 50 gallons of water for drinking, bathing, cooking, and maintenance. Most people, however, are unaware of the source of their water. In the United States, about 88 percent of the population is supplied by community water supply systems. The other 12percent is supplied by non-community means, such as campgrounds, resorts, and private wells. Sixty-four percent of public water systems use surface water as their source, the other 36 percent use groundwater from wells. The aesthetic properties of the drinking water from these public systems is often affected by the source of the water. Groundwater often has a slightly metallic taste and may contain high amounts of minerals. Surface waters, on the other hand, usually have a musty taste and look cloudy. Treatment Techniques aim to produce a water that is: safe for human consumption; appealing

and good tasting to the consumer; and conforms with applicable State and Federal regulations at the lowest possible cost.

Evil people in Whitehouse

America has a lot of evil people controlling our lives in the Whitehouse and the government. Why is all the good Christians in government letting this country be controlled by the Evil ones. We have turned this country into Sodom and Gomorrah, our hearts have turned to stone. There is no soulful music to make our hearts feel love, just rap music that makes our hearts feel hatred and pain.

Fake News by Russia

Man, the Russian's are brilliant to come up with the fake news, so that the American electoral voters, failed for this negativism in the election. So, guess who first alerted us to the fake news schemes, your president "TRUMP", proves he had to know about it.!

BLACK HISTORY

BLACK HISTORY! A SALUTE TO ALL THE BLACKS SLAVES WHO DIED FOR OUR FREEDOM, AND TO ALL THE BLACK CIVIL WAR SOLDIERS,INCLUDING WORLD WAR I AND II.ALSO TO ALL THE CIVIL RIGHTS LEADERS WHO DIED FOR OUR CIVIL RIGHTS!C'EST LA VIE

Proud Mary's

Let these truths be self-evidence, a salute to all the great grand moms, and grandmoms of color in America. Now the white women whom for centuries let their white men harass and rape and kill out women of color in the past. White woman you are just getting the same treatment that you let happen to us for centuries, by turning the other cheek and looking out the window. These white men were horrible then and still is now. But you never cared one bit about the harassment and rape doing your freedom to just say I am not going to allow another human being to be treated this way. My grandmother was one of those women getting molested by one of the wealthiest white men in this country. He was the son of a tobacco plantation owner. So I don't feel sorry for any of you selfish white females. Let us salute all the women of color who had to endure this injustice for centuries. This was "These were Proud Mary's!

Labeling of Religion

Well Mr. Trump you have awaken the conscious of white America, whether they are labeled Muslim immigrants, Christian immigrants or whatever they call themselves, now they can feel the sting of discrimination, something we blacks had to put up with for hundreds of years. Knowing that the white race violates and discriminate with one's race because the color of ones skin! Now they are discriminating with you because of your religion. Most of this country is immigrants, Jews, Muslims, Christians, etc.

Spirit of God Spirit of God

When you go to church today, take the spirit of GOD with you, and bring the spirit of God backout the door, and not the spirit of the leader on the pulpit! God is within you, heart, mind, and soul! You control your destiny

U.S. tax dollars

How is it that this country is sending our tax dollars over to foreign countries and for what? Most of these countries such as Israel has socialist democracy and live better than we do.

Difference in Race vs Culture

What is the difference between a Negro American and a Negro Latino? The only difference is their language and where they originated from. Mr. President don't get it twisted!

Equality

America has failed to recognize that all men are created "EQUAL" and should be treated "EQUAL".

Negroid

Did you know the NEGROID RACE is BI-RACIAL! So why is it the whites when currently mating with our race act like this is something new? Duh!!!!!!!!!!!!!!!!!!!This is what happened when the plantation owners was raping our AFRICAN women!!!!!!!!!!!!!!!!!!

Tribes

The only people who mention the word "Tribes" is black people. So, does this make you believe we are the tribes that existed in the bible? We are the first and the original humans!

Manhood and Womanhood

Word for today, don't let anyone smother out your manhood or womanhood because it will make you very stressed and that is not good for your health, you got to make some people who can't plan for themselves stand up and do it for themselves to take the pressure off you! It is not about love, it is about equal opportunity to do for oneself!

Spirit of GOD

When you go to church today, take the spirit of GOD with you, and bring the spirit of God back out the door, and not the spirit of the leader on the pulpit! God is within you, heart, mind, and soul! You control your destiny!

Government shutdown

HOW CAN WE HAVE A GOVERNMENT SHUT DOOR,WHEN WE VOTED AND PUT THESE POLITICIANS IN THE WHITEHOUSE TO KEEP THE COUNTRY SAFE AND RUNNING!WE NEED TO VOTE ALL THEIR SELFISH ASSES OUT IN THE NEXT ELECTION,THIS INCLUDES THE PRESIDENT.THEY ARE ALL SELFISH AND UNPATRIOTIC!WE NEED A ONE PARTY SYSTEM,THAT'S ALL FOR ONE AND ONE FOR ALL IN AMERICA!WE THE CITIZENS ARE BENEFITTING FROM ONE POLICY THAT THEY HAVE CREATED AND VOTED ON!

Black men and Black female relationships

You know my study of black men and black female relationships. When you marry and accumulate children by a woman. Then you divorce and sooner or later you meet someone else. Then you have another child. Why is it the woman become enemies? If this was a white situation, they all learn to love and let live one another as one big happy family for the children's sake. So, I ask myself why we can't as black woman grow and become understanding to the needs of embracing each other as a family, even the children need one another and they watch how the parents react. I am saying this as to say this is what's wrong with the blackface hate one another because things are not going our way, but we can make it right by embracing one another just like the other races do in their time of need!

Russia's Assimilates in America

RUSSIA IS USING TRUMP TO ASSIMILATE THEIR WHITE RUSSIAN IMMIGRANTS INTO THE AMERICAN CULTURE,WHICH WILL ALLOW FOR THEIR DYSFUNCTIONS TO ACCOMPANY THEM.JUST LIKE CLINTON AND BUSH ASSIMILATED THE ARAB-CHALDEANS INTO AMERICAN CULTURE,WHICH ALLOWED THEM TO TAKE OVER THE BLACK MAN'S MINORITY STATUS THAT OUR CIVIL RIGHTS LEADERS ACCOMPLISHED FOR OUR COMMUNITIES!NOW ON TOP OF INSULTS CALLING PERSONS OF COLOR FROM THE CARIBBEAN'S' SHITHOLES' SHOULD OPEN UP YOUR EYES THAT THIS PRESIDENT IS STRIVING FOR A PURE WHITE AMERICA!SO LIBERALS WAKE YOUR ASSES UP!

Veterans

Question to Veterans? If America politicians ask you to go fight a war with, let's say Russia, and at the same time have a open door immigration policy. Then why are you giving up your life and family to satisfy these silly fucking politicians? The war with Iraq, only made it better for the people to come over to America and become rich in the black neighborhoods. All that killing and for what!!!!!And who suffers, the veterans and the black poor communities!

Martin Luther King

It's great listening at our dear "MARTIN LUTHER KING", AND IT IS GREAT TO COME TOGETHER AS A PEOPLE AND RAISE UP AND GO INTO ACTION, FORMING GROUPS TO INFORM AND MAKE OUR RACE STRONGER, AND KINDER TO EACH OTHER., AND THIS STARTS AT HOME WITH OUR CHILDREN.MAKE THEM INDEPENDENT, BUT DON'T KICK THEM TO THE CURB.IT IS HARDER THAN EVER TO RAISE A CHILD,ESPECIALLY AS A SINGLE PARENT!!!

Leaders

How can a man lead the country that has been a melting pot since time has begun and disrespect the American people (White and Black) that he governs over!

POOR VS WEALTHY

Why is it a small group of people(wealthy), who don't want the majority of humans (poor, middle class) to live like what GOD intended it to be. They want us to beg and plead for things that are an inherited GOD given right, just to live and be happy! Let's collectively by voting run them out of high places! Let's stop self-destruction because they want us to live in poverty and bad health!

Desocialization/Criminalizing

THE DESOCIALIZATION AND CRIMINALIZING OF NEGRO'S IN AMERICA AND AROUND THE WORLD HAS FINALLY CAME TO BARE FRUIT UPON OUR PEOPLE AND COMMUNITIES!

Decriminalize Yourself

BLACKMAN STAND UP AND SOCIALIZE AND DECRIMINALIZE YOURSELF FROM SELF HATRED, POVERTY, AND EDUCATE YOURSELF FROM THE ADDICTIONS THAT BRING YOU DOWN, IN ORDER TO LIFT YOURSELF UP!

Rapping vs Singing

There is no soulfulness joy to "Rapping", we must start "Singing" again to communicate with our souls to bring unity and peace, within our communities! This is how the Whiteman is controlling the young black minds. The "Rapping" is stopping our communication with each other, but "Singing" brings out the soulfulness that the "Messiah" intended for us to keep us in unity with his spirit!

Electoral votes

We as Americans have entrusted our lives within the hands of a voting system, which has been compromised by the electoral voting and the people who cast their electoral votes and not the popular vote of what the people want. No one at this point has requested an investigation of how in the world the electoral votes, choose Donald Trump, as we see every day this president does not need to be in the Whitehouse because of his bi-polar tendencies that he displays in his tweeting, and is not professional at all in his current apprenticeship job of being a president.

TO BE CONTINUED.DEDICATED TO PEACE

THE AWAKENING OF KAFFEINE KOFFEE

ABOUT THE AUTHOR

THE AUTHOR HAS ALWAYS BEEN ASSOCIATED WITH HOW THE WORLD SURVIVES, AND HOW WE CAN MAKE IT BETTER! HER MAIN INTEREST HAS BEEN IN THE SOCIALIZATION OF MANKIND.SHE HAS DEDICATED HER LIFE INTO FOSTERING AND ADOPTING CHILDREN THAT WAS REMOVED FROM THEIR HOMES IN THE CITY OF DETROIT,MICHIGAN.SHE WORKED TIRELESSLY AT MDHHS TO HELP PROVIDES SERVICES FOR THE POOR AND INDIGENT.HER ACCOMPLISHMENTS HAVE BEEN IN RAISING A FAMILY AND ADOPTING CHILDREN SINGLE HANDEDLY,UNTIL SHE RETIRED FROM SOCIAL SERVICES IN 2004.

FUTURE BOOKS BY THE AUTHOR

2008-2012 THE AWAKENING OF KAFFEINE KOFFEE

2013-2013 THE AWAKENING OF KAFFEINE KOFFEE

2014-2016 THE AWAKENING OF KAFFEINE KOFFEE

2016-2018 THE AWAKENING OF KAFFEINE KOFFEE

2019-2020 THE AWAKENING OF KAFFEINE KOFFEE